1

Three Days with David

By

Karen Faszcza

Copyright 2015 by Karen Faszcza

Published by Karen Faszcza

This is a work of non-fiction. To protect the privacy of those involved, all names have been changed.

ACKNOWLEDMENTS

Many thanks go to Betsy Conz, my personal friend that helped me with much editing of this story. Betsy teaches at an Elementary school in Greenfield.

My deepest appreciation and sincere thanks go to my great friend Joe Bartolomeo, who so generously gave his time to do the final edit and correct the grammatical errors in my story.

Joe is a Professor at the University of Massachusetts, and I cannot thank him enough for volunteering his personal time and expertise to my project.

I also want to thank my friend Penny Robbins. She so graciously donated her time to read my many drafts and suggested several creative improvements. Penny is a free-lance writer and private English tutor to many area college students.

My enormous thanks go to my new friend, Richard Alan Smith who so graciously helped me with his technical support. I learned so much from him. I couldn't possibly have done this on my own. Richard has published three books, A Sailors Haiku, A House of Words, and Emergency Deep: One Man's Life in the Submarine Service. He is currently working on his fourth book.

I want to thank John W. for his patience, and his help in my search for David. Without John, finding David might not have been possible.

To my family, I want to thank my husband, Jerry, my daughters, Kristine, Jessica and Jillian, my sisters, Wendy and Marilyn, and my brothers, Timothy and Michael, for the encouragement and support they all gave me in my search for David.

Introduction

Three days with David is a true story of my life. It's the story of the relationships with the three men in my life, my mother, my siblings and friends. It is a love story, and in its own way, a ghost story.

This adventure also includes two of the three cancers I was diagnosed with and how they affected me. Looking over my life's experiences, I suppose it's also the story of how my faith, hope, and inspiration blossomed. These life lessons, journeys and spiritual guidance helped me to become the person that I am. Not perfect by any means, but constantly learning and accepting of the choices I have made.

I want to introduce you to these wonderful but very human people in my life. I will also share some of the most personal moments of my life. I will share this story with all the humor, love, and truth that it deserves.

I found that writing of my life's experiences, especially of my late childhood and teenage years, brought on very strong emotions. So strong, that I kept a box of tissues close to my side. Never having gone through the process of writing a memoir, imagine my shock of turning into a blubbering idiot when summoning the past. Yes, even I was surprised. Unexpectedly, I also found myself switching gears to giggling and laughter over the foolish things I would try to get away with. Being so young, I could not fully understand the consequences of my actions, and the more dire ones at that.

My perceptions of myself, especially during my teenage years were quite off the wall. Naivety and inexperience were in an endless supply during those difficult years. Reason and logic flew out the window. Of course, this is all part of the growing up years.

I always thought my father was overly strict with me. I never realized that my own actions as an adult would mimic my father's style of parenting. I wouldn't understand the emotions and protective instincts I would feel for my children, until I became a parent myself.

It is my desire that this memoir will have some helpful information and perhaps some inspirational messages for those who may need them. Overall, I hope this memoir of some of my life's experiences, will be enjoyable to all those who read it.

Chapter 1

The alarm clock rang, but I didn't want to get out of bed. I felt so tired; I had another restless night's sleep. Images kept dancing in my head. Memories of the past kept repeating themselves. Was I dreaming? Was it something else? What could this be? Why did it keep happening? I closed my sleepy eyes and drifted off to sleep for just a few minutes when suddenly I heard Jerry toot his car horn to say goodbye. I jumped out of bed in a panic that I would be late for work.

I ran into the bathroom to brush my teeth then quickly jumped into the shower. As the warm water was cascading down my face, I began to think about the dream. It was so easy to get lost in the dream. I wish I knew what it all meant. I turned off the water, grabbed my towel, and dried off my weight-gained body.

"Ugh."

There was a time when I felt proud of my figure. Even after my third daughter was born, I got down to five pounds above my pre-pregnancy weight. Now twenty-one years later, I felt like an elephant.

Okay, Karen, get over it. Grab that magic face moisturizer and doctor yourself up.

I blew dried my hair, put on my make-up, ran into my closet, pulled off the freshly ironed burgundy scrubs from the rack, threw on my uniform, socks and sneakers, then ran down stairs to start a pot of coffee. I quickly poured my cereal into a bowl and added my 1% milk. Then I poured the coffee into my large silver travel mug adding two packets of Splenda and Half and Half. I threw on my sweater and ran out the door. As I got into my car, I thought again of David, the focus of my dreams.

It was another busy day at work. We had forty six patients scheduled. The medical office was a never ending, fast-paced, and understaffed Gastroenterology office that had outgrown its space. The staff, providers, and patients, however, helped make the days worthwhile with the witty and sometimes crazy antics that were displayed from time to time. The morning flew by. I had twenty five minutes left of my hour lunch, just enough time to run across the street to Coop's to buy a sandwich. I ordered a tuna salad on wheat with lettuce no tomato. I grabbed a bottle of raspberry seltzer, paid at the register and quickly returned to the office, to eat at my desk.

The last patient of the day had left the office. My charting was nearly completed and the schedules and charts were prepped for the following day. Today's work was done.

Although I was tired, I had a few errands to run before going home. I couldn't wait to get home to change into my jams, put my feet up and relax before dinner. As I rounded the corner to my home, my car radio played *our song*... Diana Ross singing "Ain't No Mountain High Enough." Suddenly my mind drifted off to David. Memories of long ago were rushing through my mind. I had been so in love with him. I often sang this song to him, swearing I would always go to him whenever, if ever, he needed me. I pulled into the garage and continued to listen to the end of the song. My mind was so absorbed that I didn't notice Jerry had beaten me home.

As I walked into the house the smell of Jerry's infamous chili met me at the door. Thank you God, I whispered to myself. My feet were killing me and I didn't have to cook.

"Where were you?" Jerry asked.

"I told you I might be working late," I said.

"You didn't say you would be this late," said Jerry, as he hugged me.

"Sorry, the grocery store was busier than I expected."

After cleaning the dishes and watching a little television, I found myself falling asleep on the sofa. Despite the early hour, I kissed my husband and daughter Jill goodnight and went upstairs to bed. Tomorrow morning would be here soon enough and I needed to catch up on my rest. I brushed my teeth, washed my face, crawled into bed and turned off the light. I was so tired.

Dear God, please let me get a good night sleep. You know I need it.

When the alarm rang, it was six a.m. and Jerry was getting out of bed. He asked me why I was standing and looking out of the bedroom window again. I responded that I had another dream.

Confused, and somewhat shaken, I crawled back into bed to try to catch one more hour of rest before starting another work day. Needless to say, I could not fall asleep. David clung to my thoughts and the mystery continued.

That day was a light day at the office. One of the three providers on my team had procedures at the hospital all day, so I was able to keep up on my charting and paperwork. The phone at my desk rang, and Amy, one of the receptionists, said,

"Karen, you have a call from your Dad."

I pushed the button to receive his call, knowing something was wrong. Dad never called me at work.

"Hi honey" he said. "Sorry to bother you, but your Aunt Mary died this morning."

He went on to say, he went to the funeral home with my Uncle Jim to help him with the arrangements. The calling hours would be Friday night and Saturday would be the Mass and burial. I was somewhat stunned at the news, but my aunt had heart problems and had two open heart-surgeries.

"I can't say I am shocked. Jerry and I will be there, Dad. See you tomorrow night."

Chapter 2

Jerry and I attended Aunt Mary's wake. All of my nine cousins and their children were there along with my Uncle Jim. My two brothers and one of my two sisters were able to attend the service. Dad and Lorraine had left the funeral home just before we arrived. It had been many years since I'd seen several of my cousins, and as nice as it was to get together, it was difficult under the circumstances. Not to mention that my hometown, family, and friends again reminded me of David and the dream.

As Jerry and I were leaving the wake, I had a chance to ask my younger brother Tim if he had seen or knew anything of David White. Tim gave me a funny look and asked me why I was asking about David.

"Oh, you wouldn't believe me if I told you."

"Try me", Tim said.

"It was really silly, Timmy. I'm not sure I could explain it."

Jerry jumped into the conversation and said with the roll of his eyes,

"She's been dreaming about him."

"Dreaming about him?" asked Tim.
"What's with that? Why would you dream about David? Are you and Jerry having problems? How long have you been married now? Thirty three years?"

I said, "NO, we're not having problems, and that's not the point!"

 "Okay, what then?" asked Tim.

"He's been haunting my dreams for the last year or two, and I can't figure out why. I was wondering if he was okay, or, if he….died?"

Tim had no idea. He hadn't seen nor heard from David in many years. He said he would let me know if he found anything out.

That next day we attended the funeral. The Mass was as lovely as any funeral mass could be. It brought back the sad memories of losing my mother, Mary L. O'Reilly (yes, another Mary) so many years ago. My mom was forty-two years young, when she died of lung cancer. She left behind my father Douglas, my two sisters Wendy and Marilyn, my brothers Tim and Mike, and of course, me. I was the oldest of the five kids, and attending Aunt Mary's service was a sad reminder of the painful loss we shared.

Three weeks had passed since Aunt Mary's funeral and I continued to have the dreams of David. I felt more concerned than ever about them. I told Jerry.

I am really beginning to worry about this; I feel he is in trouble. Something strange is happening.

Later that day, I called Tim to ask him if he found out anything about David. He had not. I was on my own.

Chapter 3

I decided to see if David was listed in the phone book. I found his number and address listed in the small New England town where I grew up. After visiting my Dad and step mom Lorraine the next day, I drove to the street where I believed David and his wife lived. I did not see anyone nor could I tell if anyone was home. I was not about to knock on the door, so I just drove away and began the forty minute drive back to my home in Hamp.

Two more weeks went by and I went back to see my Dad again. After the visit, I decided to take another drive down David's street, even though it was getting dark. I noticed a truck in the driveway. I saw a man standing near the truck, but I could not see who it was. *It's now or never*, I told myself. I had to seize the moment or it may be lost forever. I pulled over and parked my car. I got out, and then called out.

"David, is that you?"

"Yes" he said.

I asked him if I could speak with him for a moment. He started to walk towards me. As he approached, he looked taller than I remembered and I quickly realized this was not David White.

"I'm so sorry", I said. I was looking for David A. White."

The young man said he was David's son, David Jr. I introduced myself to him, saying I was a neighbor of the White family that lived on Morgan Circle. I told this young David I had known his Dad well (not mentioning that we had been engaged) and that I grew up with his Uncle John and Aunt Cindy. Young David told me his father was not there. David said his parents were divorced, and that his father had moved to Florida several years ago. David said he hadn't heard from his Dad in all those years, and didn't know where in Florida he lived. *Whoa*, I thought. *What could make a man so distant from his family?*

It did not surprise me to learn from David Jr. that his grandfather, Arnold, had died. I had learned years ago, when I had stopped to visit the White family one summer day, that his grandmother Mary (yes, three Mary's) had died from lung cancer as my mother had. I was quite shocked and sad to learn from David Jr. that his Aunt Cindy had also died from cancer. He did not know where his Uncle John was. We chatted a little more. He then said he did not have any other information, so I thanked him for his time and apologized for bothering him. He was so polite and very kind to tell me it was no bother at all.

I now knew that David was presumably in Florida and that his Brother John's whereabouts were not known. Something was happening though. Exactly what, I wasn't sure; but I did know that I needed to continue to search for David. The dreams were real and I had a stronger belief more than ever that he needed help...*my* help!

Chapter 4

It began during the summer of 1965.
David was the oldest of three kids, and lived
with his parents Mary and Arnold White, his
brother John, and his little sister Cindy.
That was an exciting summer for me
because I had such a wild crush on David.
The more time we spent together, the harder
I fell for him. I feared my dreams of being
with him would come crashing down on me,
if he discovered my real age. But until that
happened, I tried so hard to act older than I
was. I wanted to keep my secret as long as I
could.

I was just thirteen, the first time I saw
David. He had moved into my
neighborhood just five houses from mine. I
thought he was so cute. It wasn't long before
I developed quite a crush on him. David was
my first crush. He was not only cool, but
handsome and very popular among the girls.

School had let out for the summer. I would
be entering the eighth grade in the fall. One
Saturday night in June, David was
babysitting for his brother and sister. I was
returning from a friend's house down the

street. As I walked past his house, he called out to me. He was sitting on his front porch.

I went back to talk with him and, of course, flashed him a shy smile. He was listening to his favorite records. We started talking, but I don't think I heard what he had to say. I just stared at his beautiful blue eyes. Then I remembered we started to talk about our favorite records and artists. As we talked he leaned over and kissed me. I must have gasped, and blushed, a little, because he smiled and put his hands around the back of my neck, pulled me close to him, and kissed me again. I nearly lost my breath. Despite the butterflies inhabiting my stomach, I kissed him back while hearing the music in the background of the Beach Boys "In My Room."

Yes, I was thirteen, but I lied when he asked me my age. I said I was fourteen. I knew he'd never look at me if he knew my real age. David was seventeen, had very dark brown hair, (almost black) and the most beautiful blue eyes with long dark eyelashes. He was about two inches taller than me   He was so handsome that to look at him made my heart skip beats.

David would stop by to see me from time to time. We'd listen to records while sitting in my basement family room. I still laugh when I think of one time when we were in the family room with the lights dimly lit, dancing to Franks Sinatra's "Strangers in the Night." My mother kept walking down the stairs to turn the lights up. As soon as she walked up the stairs, David would turn the lights down again. After repeating this routine several times, my mom booted us out of the house. She had a smile on her face, so I knew she wasn't really angry, but simply protective of me. My father, on the other hand, would have shot David. Okay, not really, but David would have been sent home and *I* would have been grounded.

"Good Lord," I prayed, *"when I have kids, please don't let me be as hard on them as my Dad is with me."*

I couldn't understand why my father was so strict with me. I wouldn't have done anything wrong. I was sure I would have more trust in my kids than my Dad seemed to have with me.

Now and then I would stop over to see David, especially when he was working on his car in his front yard. I would sit quietly on his front steps to watch him. He was very mechanically inclined. He had a love for cars and worked on them every chance he got. I was not allowed to ride in cars, but David and I would walk, hand in hand to the park near our home, to spend some time alone.

Cindy and John were often invited to swim at the new pool my Dad had built, and since their parents were working, David would be their designated life guard. O'Reilly's pool rules mandated that all kids had to have an older sibling or parent with them when they swam. Gee, how convenient was that for me? I loved those rules!

That summer flew by so quickly. Just before school started, my world finally crashed. David found out I was thirteen. He was not happy to discover my lie, which I confessed to one night prior to the school year starting. I knew I had to tell him the truth or he would certainly learn of it at his school. He was really annoyed with me as I tried so hard to explain my reason for lying. I told him I was afraid he wouldn't be interested in me if he knew my real age.

"You're right about that." he said.

Needless to say, the school year began and I did not see David, at least not in the way I wanted to see him. He of course would drive by and wave, but always had a girl sitting beside him. My heart would break each time I saw him with another girl, My Dad would always say,

"It's just a crush. You'll get over it."

I would look at my mom with tears in my eyes and she would smile and say,

"What is meant to be will be, honey."

The school year seemed endless but it did come to an end, and a brand new summer was upon us. I had just celebrated my fourteenth birthday. Although this last school year made demands on David and me, pulling us in different directions, once summer began, we found ourselves in each other's company.

My sister Wendy, three years younger than I, was my best friend and ally. She often tried to cover for me when I was visiting with David, instead of being with my girlfriends as my parents believed. But she was smart enough to hold it over my head when she wanted a favor! My younger siblings were too young to understand or *even care* about my crush on David.

David had graduated from Vocational High School that past June. After his graduation ceremony, David told me he was planning on going into the service. He asked if I thought he should go into the Navy or the Air Force. I told him that if it was up to me, I would like to see him join the Air Force for purely selfish reasons. Westover Air Force Base was nearby.

Chapter 5

Summers were the best time for David and me to get together. Carefree days were spent swimming in my family pool, or going for walks to the park. Sometimes I would manage to sneak over to his house when he was babysitting for John and Cindy. My Dad would have had my head if he knew I was there without his parents at home. My parents were very strict with us kids. Being the oldest of five children, I was always expected to set a "good example."

We had such fun on those hot summer nights, when David, my friends, and I would be swimming in our pool. I remember how refreshing the water felt and the sound of the crickets chirping in the tall grass. It wasn't the underwater tag we would play, that was so exciting. It was sneaking kisses, right under my parents' noses.

Sometimes at night, David and I would sit on the front porch with our friends and talk a lot about nothing. We had fun just sitting and telling jokes or counting the stars and even catching fireflies. Another summer was coming to an end. It was getting dark early in the evening, and of course, my dad would call me in the house early.

At fifteen I would think my Dad would have given me some leeway and allow me the privilege of staying out with the other kids. But, no. He had to be the authoritative figure that would always spoil my fun. I didn't realize at the time my Dads authoritative stance was out of love and concern for *me*, his *fifteen year old daughter.*

David did enlist in the Air Force late that summer, and soon he was off to Lackland Air Force Base in Texas for training. He promised to write me and I looked for his letters. I treasured each letter I received and would promptly write back.

Chapter 6

In September, I entered my sophomore year at the high school. Public school was quite liberating compared to Catholic school. I was meeting new kids and going to dances. I became very active in many school programs. I spent many weekends horseback riding with friends. Keeping busy helped to keep my mind off of David. In fact I dated off and on and on occasion developed a crush or two. I missed David while he was off to Basic training with the Air Force.

David came home on his first leave. He looked so handsome in his dress uniform. There was something about a man in a uniform, and to me, David was so incredibly handsome. While he was on leave, we spent most of our time together at his house with his family.

I still tried every trick in the book to see David when I could, my parents would occasionally allow me to ride with David in his car now that I had entered my high school years. We would go to the Root Beer Stand or Friendly's Ice Cream Shoppe for a bite to eat, but other than those few times,

David and I didn't spend much time alone. My parents were so "old fashioned." His leave seemed too short. Before I knew it, he was off to Colorado Springs for his next training program.

One night in February, while David was still in Colorado, my Mom called me into her bedroom. She told me Mary White called her to tell her that David met a girl and was planning on getting married. Mary asked my Mom to break the news to me. I was crushed by this devastating news. I had no idea he was seeing anyone seriously. But then again I was dating even though David was always in my heart. I thought he felt the same. Soon after this heartbreaking news, I went over to visit with David's mom. She was very understanding and a big comfort to me. She believed in her heart, David was being impulsive, and that he was homesick and lonesome. My visit with Mrs. White gave me hope. Once again I was reminded by my mom and David's mom that "what's meant to be, will be." Fortunately for me, their romance ended.

I prayed like crazy that his assignment after his graduation would be stateside or in Germany, and God forbid *not* Viet Nam. David wrote me to tell me he would be going to Guam. His primary assignment was to service B-52s that flew bombing missions over Viet Nam. He also volunteered to fly many of those missions.

David returned from Guam after nine long months. When I saw him I jumped into his arms and thanked God for his safe return. We saw each other as much as we could, but my Dad was still against me officially dating or going steady with him. Although David's next assignment was to Westover, I did not get to be with him as often as I hoped. We did date other people, although we did manage to sneak dates in now and then. I was still crazy about him and was certain he felt the same way.

Once more David was assigned an overseas tour. This time he was to be stationed in Okinawa, Japan. I was now in my junior year of high school and again had to say goodbye to him. On the morning he was to leave, I walked over to his house before school began so I could see him one more time. This goodbye was so difficult. I sobbed in his arms as he held me close. I couldn't stop crying. I was so afraid. I couldn't bear to let him go; but had no choice.

"No tears." he kept saying.

As hard as I tried, I could not keep the tears from flowing down my cheeks. God, why did there have to be a war? Why did our country have to be involved in Viet Nam? It wasn't fair, it wasn't right. He kissed me goodbye and drove off in the car to join his unit back at Westover before flying to Okinawa. We wrote frequent letters and I would fall more in love with David with each letter I received.

Chapter 7

That year my family moved to a new home. In the three years since my sister Marilyn was born, my family had outgrown our three bedroom house with the pool on Morgan Circle. My parents looked for a new home and found one about a fifteen-minute walk from my neighborhood. I was devastated none the less. I loved the pool, I loved my childhood friends, I loved my neighborhood, and most of all I loved living so close to David and his family. We were moving into a six bedroom three and a half bath colonial with more than enough room for each member of my family. I didn't care. I wanted to be near my friends and, my second family, the Whites. After the move, I did continue to visit with David's family as often as possible.

Another year went by; David and I exchanged letters almost daily. I can still see the closing of each letter that ended with

"May God keep you safe till I get home. Love always," David.

God did keep me safe, God kept David safe, but not everybody was safe. I went to take my final exams my junior year of high school, only to find out that the boyfriend and brother of two of my classmates was killed when he stepped on a land mine in Viet Nam. It was such a sad day. Our entire class was shaken. I prayed even harder that David would come home safely and soon.

David arrived at Westover Air Force base. I was thrilled to ride with his family to greet him along with his fellow Airmen. I ran up to him once again, jumping into his arms. He was home. *Thank God!*

I had one more school year before I turned eighteen, then I would be able to date David steadily after I graduated from high school.

Chapter 8

The summer, of 1970, I finally graduated.
David and I spent nearly every night
together that we could. I was in heaven. I
was with the one I loved and he loved me.
Much of our time was spent at his house. He
never felt very comfortable around my Dad,
so staying at my house was rare. David was
nine months away from discharge from the
service and was lucky enough to live off
base with his family.

We were homebodies for the most part; but
occasionally we would go to a movie or out
to eat. One Saturday night, we went to see
some silly beach movie at the drive-in with
some friends. After the movie, we dropped
off our friends, and went for a drive. I
remember we had stopped near the
mountaintop to talk about our future. We
wanted to get married, but I would be
starting at the community college in the fall
and he still had months left in the service.

It was very hard for us not to become
intimately involved. I really wanted to wait
until we were married before that happened.
At times when we were alone, we would end
up arguing because I fought any intimate

desire I had. Sometimes the temptation was so overwhelming that I would try to break the intense moments with some humor. I remember one night while we were parked up on the mountain, I asked David if he wanted to get into the back seat of the car. You never saw anyone fly over the seat so fast. As he sat in the back, he asked,

"Well, are you going to join me?"

I said, "No, I didn't say I wanted to go back there; I asked if you wanted to go back there."

We laughed so hard, but at least I was able to maintain control and not lose my senses, as I was so close to doing.

September began and I started my freshman year at the community college in our home town. David asked me to marry him. My dream had come true! We were unofficially engaged and tentatively planned our wedding date for the following September. By then, David would have completed his commitment with the Air Force by the end of February. That gave David several months to find a job. We needed to find an apartment and plan our wedding.

I was so in love with him, and had been since junior high school. I not only loved him, but his family as well. My relationship with them had grown immensely, having spent so many evenings visiting with them while David was overseas. My friendship with his mother and family was more special than anyone could have known. They truly were my second family.

David's parents knew that David was about to give me the long awaited diamond ring, and were very excited to learn we were now officially engaged. My father on the other hand, was quite reserved. He looked deeply into my eyes and said with a stern voice,

"Are you sure this is what you want? Marriage is forever, so be sure before you walk down the aisle."

I did not feel supported by my Dad. It unnerved me more than I wanted to admit. There was something Dad did not share with me that would leave me with spiraling doubts. One could say I was blinded by love because there were some changes in David that I was not willing or able to see.

Periodically, I would scour through the newspapers to help David find work. My father had many friends with businesses who had offered various jobs to David, but for one reason or another, he was not interested in those jobs at the time. I was beginning to worry about David's unemployment. Mary White would say,

"Don't worry, Karen. He will be out of the service soon. Give him some time. He will find something."

I tried to accept her words, but was worried none-the-less.

The following months were quite busy. I was trying so hard to balance school, my part time job at the department store, and my time with David. The holidays and semester finals were approaching faster than expected. I got through my first semester of classes with decent grades but could have done better. I felt such relief when winter break came. I worked extra hours at Weston's Department Store and spent most of my free time with David.

Although I didn't believe in pre-marital sex, as passionately in love as we were, it became impossible not to consummate our love before the wedding rings went on our fingers. In the heat of one sultry and all-consuming night, David introduced me to the passion and romance of making love. I had never experienced such intense physical feelings as I did on that night. I was not quite sure what was happening to my body, but as nervous as I was, I loved every moment we shared. Words could not express what I was feeling. I just knew that I was forever tied to David through the bond of our love.

This was the beginning of the most exciting time of my life. I was engaged. I had a wedding dress to look for, bridesmaids to choose, dishes to pick out, and flowers to select. Although we had not found an apartment, we did start to pick out some furniture.

Every week, we would visit with David's best friend from high school and his wife. David would pick me up at 7 PM and we would go over to Tony and Donna's, a young married couple with a beautiful two year old daughter. We would bring soda and beer over, make popcorn, and watch television. We always left by 10 PM as they had to work the next day and I had classes. David was no longer in the Air Force, and was still looking for work.

A pattern, so it seemed, was beginning to develop. Many nights, I would be at home waiting for David to pick me up. He would show up late or sometimes not at all. He would call later to apologize and I would ask,

Where the hell have you been?

"I was at the bar with some friends..." he would say, "and lost track of time."

He was drinking more and more.

While sitting in my family's kitchen after dinner one night, I asked Wendy to be my Maid of Honor. She looked at me as if I had two green heads.

"NO!" she said.

"What do you mean by that?" I asked.

"No, I won't be in your wedding. I don't like David and you're stupid to marry him."

"What the hell does that mean," I asked.

"You're an idiot, Karen. David is lying to you; he cheats on you and is drunk most of the time!"

Chapter 9

How quickly one night can change your whole life: This was supposed to be the most exciting time of my life. Instead it became the opposite. I didn't understand why things were changing but they were. David and I began to argue. I realized he spent too much time drinking with his friends. My grades at college were slipping. I wasn't happy with my classes. I wasn't happy with David. I loved David with all my heart, but I was not happy. David seemed to be more interested in his friends. He seemed to be more interested in his beer. We were six months away from our wedding and he did not have a job. How were we to afford an apartment and support ourselves? He was unemployed and I was a full-time student with a part-time job. Why was this happening?

The arguing continued. I had had enough. I was scared. This was not my dream of my romantic life. I so feared he was becoming an alcoholic. What was I going to do? I needed some time to decide if getting married was right for us. I tried to believe that old saying "What's meant to be will be." My mom and dad could see the anguish I was going through. I was having doubts about getting married. When I mentioned to my parents that I was thinking about going away, my dad and mom agreed that getting away would be the best thing for me. My mom certainly knew my feelings for David were real, but also knew the timing was not right. She was always so wise and caring. My dad, on the other hand, was delighted I was about to break my engagement. One could see the "I told you so" look on his face.

I went to David's house to talk with him. I explained how worried I was about us. I told him things were not right. David didn't see any problem. He said I was worried about nothing. I tried to explain my fears and my feelings of insecurity, but he did not see the problem as I did. I told him he was drinking too much. He denied it. I told him that my friends saw him with other girls. He denied it. I was angry that he had stood me up or was very late on several dates. He always had an excuse. I was scared. I was confused. I was worried that getting married might be a mistake. I gave him back the engagement ring, a curve ball that he did not see coming. I was shocked to see him cry. He asked me to reconsider, but I said,

"No. Not now."

I needed time to think. I loved him. I knew that, but I was not so sure he loved me, at least not the way I needed him to love me. Although David insisted he did love me, I didn't believe he was ready to settle down.

Yes, I needed time alone and so did he. I told him I was going to go away. My close friend Judy was at college in San Francisco. Another family friend, as well as relatives, lived in or near that city. That would be my destination. I needed to get away. I couldn't stay in the same town chancing that I would run into David all the time. I had always loved David, but it apparently was not enough. It didn't prevent his drinking. I realized that he wasn't always truthful with me and he wasn't truthful with himself. I didn't know how long I would be away. I just knew I needed to put some distance between us. I dropped out of college and flew to California at the end of March. I had hoped he would realize that he did, indeed, love me and would find a way to come after me.

The Sunday morning that I left home was dreadful. I kept looking out of the living room window to see if David was outside.

He was not. Finally I got into the family car with my parents, Wendy, and my friend Pat to make the drive to Boston. The ride seemed endless. Not much was said in the car. I was afraid to speak for fear of breaking down and crying. I had cried all night as it was.

We arrived at Logan Airport, parked the car, and walked to the gate to await the arrival of my plane. It arrived. The airline agent announced we could board the plane. I kissed, hugged, and said goodbye to my mom, dad, Wendy, and dear friend Pat. I walked through the doorway that led to the plane. As I was waiting for the plane to taxi away from the gate, the pilot came over the intercom saying there was a mechanical problem with the plane. While it was being repaired, the passengers were given the option of waiting on the plane or in the terminal. Most of the passengers did go back to the gate. I did not. I knew if I stepped off that plane, I would not get back on it. So I stayed in my seat and cried.

Two hours later, the other passengers came aboard and we took off for California. It was hard to leave home. This was really my first time leaving home to go off on my own. I couldn't stop thinking about David.

Although I didn't know how long I would be away, I knew this was one of the biggest steps in my life. I needed time to sort things out. I wanted David to prove his love to me.

Chapter10

I landed in San Francisco and was met by my family friend Kathleen, and my Aunt Vi and Uncle Harry. They helped me settle into Kathleen's little apartment in the Marina section of San Francisco. I was eighteen and on my own in the city that I had become attached to when visiting my aunt and uncle when I was sixteen. Although in reality I was a guest of Kathleen, I felt like a "hot shot" living in this city on my own. I started to look for work but wasn't finding anything that suited me. I had no real experience except sales at Weston's.

I must have been in California about five or six weeks before I called David. To my surprise, he was no longer living at home with his family. No, he had also wanted to get away. He had moved to New York. Mary White gave me his phone number. I remember so clearly the call I made to him. He asked me if I was ready to come home.

"Not yet." I said. "I am really liking it here in California and want to try to work and save some money before I go back home."

I asked him how he was doing.

"OK," he said.

I wanted to tell him I still loved him. I wanted to tell him I missed him. I was so hurt from the lies and the drinking, not to mention the probable cheating, that my pride kept me quiet.

Several weeks passed and I have to say, I enjoyed living the California life. One weekend I made plans to spend time with my friend Judy at her college dorm. I took the 5 PM transit bus from the corner of Scott Street to join Judy up on Turk Blvd. I had to change buses in one of the most unpleasant parts of the city. It was 5:30 on a Friday night; I was dressed in my green and brown tweed pant suit, holding my little green overnight bag. I didn't know it then, but I was a sitting duck. It was not a safe place to be especially for a young woman alone.

After getting off the first bus, I tried to cross the street when three guys in their early twenties circled around me and asked,

"Hey baby what are you doing tonight? Come over here with us. We can have a good time."

I ran to the corner as a taxi cab pulled up very close to me. A man opened the cab door and reached out to grab me. I ran into a liquor store on that same corner in search of a safe haven. The young clerk asked if he could help me. Several other men of various ages and nationalities stood by a pinball machine in the corner of the store. They watched my every move. I was so terrified by this time I could hardly speak. I remember saying that I came in to try to find some protection. The sales clerk asked why I was in this part of the city. I told him I was going up to the college on Turk Blvd., and these were the directions I was given by the transit company. This young man, about three inches shorter than I, told me this was a very bad section of the city. So bad in fact, that the police didn't always answer distress calls. He said I would be lucky to get out alive. He also said I would be safer in the middle of Viet Nam. I was so frightened I could hardly move. I wanted to be safely at home with my family, but was in the middle of the slums of a city far from home.

God please help me! What am I going to do? Please help me get out of here."

I asked the clerk if the next bus would take me to the college. He said "yes," so I turned to walk out of the store.

As I waited on the corner for the bus, a drunken middle aged man came up to me, grabbing at me. Suddenly I heard the clerk come out of the store yelling at this drunk.

"What the hell are you doing with my girl? Can't my girl come to see me without you people bothering her?"

Hearing that, the man said,

"Sorry buddy, I didn't know she was your girl. She looks like a sweet young thing. I thought I'd show her a good time."

"Well, she is my girl, so leave her alone."

With that, I saw the bus approach. I jumped on the bus as fast as my legs could move my frozen-with-fear body, and left that God-forsaken part of the city. I never knew the name of the young man who saved me, and was sorry I never got a chance to thank him.

I shook with fear for what seemed to be hours. By the time I was met by Judy at the gates of the college, I looked as white as a ghost. I swore that from then on I would never travel to unknown areas alone. I never did, until many years later. I broke that promise to myself.

Chapter 11

My friend Judy was my anchor. After all, we had been friends since kindergarten.
While in San Francisco, I met so many young people through her. We went to many college parties. I lived the "Life of Riley."

Judy called me one Wednesday night and said,

"You've got to come up tomorrow night. Some of us girls have been invited to a party hosted by a Stanford Frat house. It's on a yacht in San Francisco Bay. I will be there!"

The bus picked us up at six and brought about twenty-five of us girls to a dock on San Francisco Bay. We met up with these nineteen to twenty-two year old guys. Judy and I were excited and nervous at the same time. We were, after all, two country bumpkins living in the "big city".

We stuck together most of the night until I met Wayne. Wayne was tall, had dark hair, dark eyes and was rather good looking. He was on crutches as a result of a broken leg. I knew I was safe with Wayne because I could always outrun him if I had to. I did not have to worry. Wayne was a real gentleman. He majored in Archeology. We had a really nice time together that night. We drank one glass of wine as I recall, and just talked about our interests and lives. He was not at all what I expected FRAT boys to be. In other words, he was very polite and not looking for a one night stand.

The night ended around 11:00 and we girls were returned safely to the college. Wayne and I said we would stay in touch, but that did not happen, as our lives were going in different directions. That was one night I would always remember. We did have a good time, He was nice. But the timing was wrong... Would I ever forget about David?

I celebrated my nineteenth birthday while living in San Francisco

Chapter 12

The next few months dragged on and still no job. Work was difficult to find. Most people were not willing to hire young transients like myself. I needed at least six months of residency to prove I would have some longevity in any job I might be offered. Since I was so new to the area, any luck in finding employment was not good. My dad was paying my bills, and I was having a great time. After five months of sunny California and no job, my dad said I'd had enough fun and had to return home. I returned to my New England town in August, just one month before what I thought was going to be my wedding.

I was home for about two weeks when I heard the startling news. My friend Pat and I were at a lake with friends one hot, sunny Sunday afternoon. I overheard a conversation about David.

"Yup, he got married, do you think she knows? "

I wanted to die ...

How could he do this to me? Did he ever really love me? Why would he get married so soon? Yet I was the one who chose to go away. I was the one asking the questions that needed to be asked before walking down the aisle. I was the one to break off the engagement. I was devastated. I remember drinking four or five glasses of wine, maybe even a full bottle after hearing that news. I cried on Pat's shoulder. What was I going to do? How could I go on? I thought my life was over.

Well, it almost was over for me when I got home and found my Mom, my Dad, Grandparents, Aunt Mary, and Uncle Jim all sitting on my front porch, watching me stagger up to the house intoxicated from drinking Boones Farm apple wine. I knew my actions would not be tolerated. I was certain I would be grounded. But much to my surprise, I learned that they were expecting some kind of outburst from me; when I learned what they already knew. Thankfully, they all seemed to understand, or at least tolerate my reaction to the news of David's marriage and let my drunkenness slide.

I needed to move on with my life. I needed to make some decisions.

What was I going to do? Go back to college? Find a job? Move back to California? I had no desire to choose any of these options, but in the end I knew I had to do something. As heartbroken as I was at hearing of David's marriage, part of me felt relieved since I still had lingering doubts. So, I found a job as a receptionist at a private school. I worked the remaining school year and planned to return to college that next September. I found a new interest in the medical field and applied to a college in a city about thirty miles from my home town.

Chapter 13

Later that year we discovered that my mother had lung cancer. She was forty one at the time of her diagnoses. She was supposed to have elective ear surgery, but that was canceled when she got the results of her pre-op chest x-ray. A spot had shown up on the x-ray that proved positive for lung cancer. Mom went to Boston for her cancer surgery. All went well, so we were told. My dad was not able to accept or believe her prognosis was terminal. His denial led us children to believe she was going to make it. We believed she would be well after her radiation treatments, which started later in the spring. We transitioned into a difficult summer. Falsely believing my mom was doing well, I was making my own plans for the summer before going back to college.

My friend Pat and I would get together with other friends and drive every Friday night up north to a place called "The Barn." It was the place to go after working all week. Many of our friends gathered together to dance and party with the great bands that played each weekend. I began to meet and date other guys. I played the field and had a blast. At least that is what I kept telling myself.

Mom was home and doing well, after the completion of her radiation treatments. Dad hired a housekeeper to help with the fourteen room house. I worked part time weekdays and partied on weekends with my friends. I would go up to mom's room to sit and talk but dad would always holler up the stairs,

"Let your mother rest!"

So, needless to say, I didn't seem to spend much time with her. When dad said jump, we jumped.

It was the end of August as I prepared to move into my new city apartment four miles from my new college. On Labor Day weekend, along with a few friends and my father, I moved my early attic furnishings up to a fourth floor walkup. The apartment was nice; it had two bedrooms, one bathroom, a dining room, living room and kitchen. It had a big front porch with a view of the courtyard. We got all of my furniture situated just so. We went to the store for some groceries, and then ordered some pizza. Then after eating, everyone left and I was alone. I was so lonesome; I could not stop thinking about David. This could have been our first apartment together.

College began and I was consumed with homework. I had classes five days a week and found a real passion for my studies. On weekends I went home to see the family and check on my mom. She was looking tired and weak, but assured me she was doing well. A few weeks later, on the second Friday afternoon of October, I went to see mom who had been admitted to the hospital. I was met at her hospital room door by my dad who said,

"You don't have to go in today, if you don't want to." "Your mom is sleeping and shouldn't be disturbed."

I said no. I wanted to sit with her for a while.

But when I went in and saw her pale sullen face, I felt sick to my stomach. She was in a coma and all I could do was look up at the ceiling. She didn't look familiar. I know that the reality of seeing her frail body due to her illness hit me very hard. I left her room, trying to hide my tears and telling my dad I was fine and would see him at home for dinner.

He came home shortly after and Dad, Wendy, Tim, Mike, Marilyn and I ate our dinner quietly. Pat came over to pick me up to go up to the Barn, but I said,

"Not tonight, Mom was not doing well."

Dad said, "Nonsense. You go. She will be alright tonight."

I tried to argue with him but he convinced to go out.

So, against my better judgement, I went. I got smashed, came home, crashed on my bed and was awakened by my dad at 6:00 AM. I looked at him with foggy eyes and saw a tear roll down his cheek. I cried and said,

"I'm sorry, Daddy!"

Mom had died about 4 a.m. alone in the hospital with no one by her side except a private nurse. I hated myself for not being with her. I hated my father for not being with her. I hated....

I was twenty at the time of her death. Wendy was seventeen, Tim fifteen, Mike twelve, and Marilyn seven. This had to be the worst experience in our lives, the loss of our mother who had celebrated her forty-second birthday just months before.

Our home began to fill with our relatives. My mother was the youngest of ten children. My aunts, uncles, and cousins came family by family with broken hearts and false smiles trying so hard to be strong for us. Mom's wake was Sunday night and she was buried on Columbus Day. There were so many friends and family who attended, I couldn't count the numbers. I was aware, however, that neither David nor his family attended the service, nor did David send a message. The death and services were so quick, that in spite of the large number who attended, there were just as many who did not attend because they did not hear of her passing in time.

I stayed home for the week, missing four days of classes. I did not want to go back to school. My father insisted I continue with school. I wanted to drop out. He would not allow it. He insisted I finish my education. He convinced me that if I quit, I would never return to college. I needed to think of my future. So, dad won. I did stay in college and finished that semester. When I returned to school in January...I met Jerry.

Chapter 14

Jerry and I dated the remainder of the school year. He was a student at a neighboring college in the same city and shared an apartment with his friend Jack. We would get together a few nights a week. He would cook dinner for me or we would go out to eat and see a movie. We were happy together and I started to look forward to each evening as we began to spend them together. It was after I graduated from college in June of 73 that I introduced Jerry to my dad and family. Jerry came to join my family for dinner on a Friday night. My Dad whipped up a fabulous seafood casserole infused with butter and garlic. It was absolutely delicious. We had a good time and I could see Jerry fitting in so comfortably with my family. After meeting Jerry that first night, my Dad told my sister Wendy that Jerry would be the one I would marry. He was right although I hadn't realized it at the time. Jerry and I became an item. We grew closer and closer every day.

The following spring, I visited David's mother. Since she had been a very special person in my life, I wanted and needed to keep in touch with my "other" family that I loved so much. I wanted to run to Mary White just after my mother's death but resisted because I thought that it would be a discourtesy to my mother. I desperately missed my mother, and I thought visiting with Mary White would be the comfort I was looking for. So after several months I did finally call her and set a date to see her.

Mary talked about David, of course. She had always hoped we would get back together. David was living in Queens, New York with his wife and stepson. She told me that David never got over me and that he had married on the rebound. He was miserable and she asked me if I would I go back with him if he left his wife? I was shocked. I couldn't believe what I was hearing. I didn't know what to say. How was I supposed to react to hearing these words when I had tried so hard to move on with my life? Suddenly I heard myself saying,

"NO!"

David was married; I wouldn't interfere in his marriage, good or bad. I believed that marriage was forever. I was falling in love with Jerry. I was moving on with my life. I found the man I knew I wanted to be with. We were building a future together. I was falling in love again. I could not and would not throw away this precious relationship.

Chapter 15

We were magic, Jerry and I! We were building a good life together, one with trust, one with laughter, and one with ever-growing love. We had known each other and dated for three years by the time we married in 1975, one year after he graduated from college. I was working in the surgical unit at a local hospital as a surgical technician. We rented a two-bedroom ranch in Jerry's home town of Hatfield for a year, before moving to Philadelphia.

It saddened me to learn that David did get his divorce. He moved back to the New England town that we grew up in, fell in love in, and broke up in. His life was not going in a good direction.

My life with Jerry in Philadelphia, however, was exciting and happy. We were a young married couple settling into a warm, spacious twin house. We really enjoyed living in the city and working at our new jobs. We met some wonderful people and were quickly making new friends. I especially appreciated the three hundred or so miles of distance between Philly and

Western MA. I felt safe and had no reminders of David.

It was good to be on our own. We worked at the same hospital, Jerry in management and I with a surgeon.

We had been married less than two years when we tried to start our family. What we thought would be an easy, natural, and intimate experience in our marriage turned out to be an unusually difficult task. Pregnancy did not come as easily as we assumed it would have. After months of trying, we saw an infertility specialist. After several tests we both endured, we found *my* problem, popped some fertility pills and BINGO, instant pregnancy. I was so ecstatic, I could hardly contain myself. Jerry and I were now entering in a new chapter of our lives.

As we learned of our pregnancy, Jerry was offered a new job with a large company back in New England. We decided moving back close to our families would be best for us. We so wanted to be near family while raising our baby. Later that year, we were blessed with our beautiful daughter Kristie; she weighed in at 5 pounds, 3 ounces, and was a tiny bit of a thing with a powerful set of lungs. We bought our first house in the small town of Florence, near the Berkshires. What joy I felt having my daughter and my loving husband, and owning our first house!

Eighteen months later, my girlfriend Pat got married. I was in her wedding, as she was in mine. She had a beautiful wedding day at the end of May. Kristie was with Jerry's mom while we were dancing at the reception. The day flew by and we were home with Kristie by early evening. I was exhausted from all the action and excitement. I decided to make it an early night.

A few weeks later, I was rushed to the hospital with an ectopic rupture. I was about four to five weeks pregnant when I started internally hemorrhaging. I nearly died. The doctor told Jerry after the surgery that they were lucky to operate when they did. I would not have survived another hour. *Someone was watching over me.* It took a while for me to get back on my feet.
I had lost so much blood, not to mention the emotional trauma I went through. But, I made it, and eighteen months later, I gave birth to our second child Jessica. She also was beautiful and she weighed in at 6 pounds, 3oz., after a ninety minute fast and

furious labor. Our family was complete, so we thought.

We had planned on two children. Jessica was two years old when a fourth pregnancy occurred, taking us completely by surprise. Sadly, as we were learning to accept the arrival and challenges of a third child, I miscarried. I was into my fourth month when I started cramping and bleeding. I was heartbroken over the loss of this unplanned pregnancy. I think I went into a mild depression.

I wanted to have another baby and was thrilled to learn Jerry felt the same way. We tried again to get pregnant but another miscarriage occurred.

Two years later, we succeeded and brought into this world a third daughter, Jillian. Jill was the easiest delivery thanks to an epidural (our first two births were natural). She weighed in at 8 pounds, 6oz, and of course, was just as beautiful as her sisters.

Now, we were complete!

Chapter 16

We bought our second house in the same town just three months before Jill was born. It didn't take long for the pressures of our jobs, a new house, and three children to upend our happy life. Jerry was traveling an hour each way to and from work. I worked two-part time jobs, took care of the girls during the day, and tried to keep up with the house. Jerry would come home from work and take over the care of our daughters while I worked evenings and weekends.

After several years, this did take a toll on our marriage. The demands of our jobs, children, house and bills almost overcame us, but with the "Grace of God," family, and friends, we were able to reset our goals and prioritize our lives. It wasn't easy, but well worth it, because family meant the world to us.

David, however, would enter my thoughts from time to time. I knew David was divorced from his first wife but wondered where he was and what he was doing Did he ever remarry? I hoped his life was a good one.

I wanted him to find happiness. I'd found it. No, marriage is not easy. Yes, Jerry and I worked through many problems, but we always loved each other and were determined to follow and honor our marriage vows. I believe that was how we overcame the challenges and difficulties in our marriage.

In spite of all that, I still thought of David, and having his love letters and pictures in the closet did not help.

I ran into David unexpectedly on two different occasions. The first time was on a Saturday morning while working a weekend job in a retail shop in town. I was speechless. The shock of seeing him was exactly that, a shock. I started to tremble and stood there with my mouth open. He was delivering some items to the store. I couldn't tell what his reaction to seeing me was because my feelings were so shaken. I wanted to hug him but I couldn't. I wanted to ask him to get a cup of coffee with me but wouldn't. That would not be right, I was married. We made small talk and we were polite, but that was all. He walked out the door. All I could do was stand there and tremble.

Several years later, chance brought us together again. I had taken my oldest daughter, Kristie, Christmas shopping at a local department store. As we turned to walk down the clothing aisle, I came face to face with David. He was not alone. He was with his second wife and eighteen month old son, David Jr. Again, I trembled but put on the friendliest smile one had ever seen. I shook hands with his wife and marveled over his son. I introduced my daughter to them. I rambled on and on about Jerry and the girls, and then said,

"Oh my, it's getting late, and I really must go. It was so nice to meet you (whatever her name was), and, of course, you look terrific, David."

They left. I wanted to throw up as Kristie and I walked down the store aisle. What was the matter with me? I had a great family. I couldn't believe my reaction to seeing him again. Was I crazy? *Get a grip Karen, he was ancient history.* I was so shaken, I lost my purse. I couldn't concentrate. When I realized my purse was missing, I tried to retrace my steps in hopes of finding it. I was lucky, though; I saw another woman with her child in tow, holding my purse. When she saw the panicked look on my face, she asked if the purse belonged to me. I nodded yes, and thanked her. I felt like such a jerk. I'd lost my purse. I tried telling myself it was better to have lost the purse than my daughter. How could I explain the events of the evening to my husband, when I couldn't explain to myself the silly reaction and nervousness I felt when running into David? Kristie and I went home; we hid the gifts we bought until we could wrap them for Christmas. I thanked God for the lady who found my purse.

I thought about David for weeks, and then one day I gathered up strength, walked up to my bedroom closet, dug out the shoe box, and threw all of his letters so nicely housed in that box into the trash. After all, I truly loved my husband and daughters, but was afraid that the reminders of David would somehow interfere with my happy life. With great reluctance, each letter was torn up along with any pictures I had of David. I felt in my heart that this was the right thing to do. So, I did it!

Christmas and New Year's passed by as quickly as they arrived. We really enjoyed the holidays. It was always such a magical time.

Chapter 17

One mid-February night, I awoke from what I thought was a dream. I was crying and standing by my bedroom window saying,

"Please don't go. Don't leave me. I need you. Don't go."

I sat on my bed trying to figure out what had just happened. My mother was there. She had sat on the edge of my bed to talk with me. She said,

"Karen, I have something very important to tell you."

She was glowing. I never saw her look so radiant or peaceful as she looked that night. We sat on the bed together, and she told me what she had to say. Then she was gone. It appeared as though she floated out of the window. That was when I found myself standing by the window crying and saying,

"Don't go!"

I recall Jerry waking and asking me what was wrong. I didn't know what to say so I told him I had a strange dream. He said,

"Come back to bed."
He put his arms around me. I lay there silently with tears in my eyes and a lump in my throat. My mother had come to tell me, something, something important, but I could not remember what she said. For weeks I felt as if I was mourning her loss again. I felt so depressed, and what was worse, I could not remember what she told me.

Six weeks later, I discovered a growth located in the front of my throat. I made an appointment with my family doctor who referred me to a surgeon. The surgeon said I had an enlarged thyroid and felt it was nothing to worry about, but we took some blood tests just the same, which turned out to be relatively normal. I returned for a follow-up visit four weeks later. The growth was larger. My surgeon suggested a biopsy. The biopsy was scheduled for two weeks after that date.

The biopsy results were positive for cancer. Now most people say if you are going to have cancer, then thyroid cancer is the easiest to cure. Uh, uh! Not in my case. The cancer I had was a follicular carcinoma. The medical books at the time indicated it was a quickly metastasizing cancer with a high mortality rate. I was approaching my forties with three daughters' age twelve, nine, and five. Was this Deja vu all over again? Was I about to repeat what had happened twenty years earlier when my mother died? No way, I was not going to die. I had three girls to raise. I was not going to leave them. I refused to leave them.

I was scheduled for a thyroidectomy at Hartford Hospital in Hartford, CT in May of 1992. Several weeks late I was at one of my doctor appointments after the surgery that I remembered what my mother had said in the "dream/visit." My mother told me that cold February night in my bedroom that I was going to be diagnosed with a cancer. She told me not to worry about it. She said I would not die from this. I would be here to raise my girls. I would not die leaving young children as she did. She said,

"I love you and I needed to tell you this to help you get through the coming months."

As I remembered this, a calmness came over me and I looked at my doctor and said,

"I'm going to be alright Henry. I'm not going anywhere. I know in my heart that I will be here to raise my children, so don't you worry. This cancer will not defeat me."

He couldn't believe my attitude and said that was just what all cancer patients needed, a positive attitude like mine. I told him it wasn't an attitude. It was a *fact*.

My pathology was reviewed a second time, and ironically, it was determined that the cancer was papillary with follicular tendencies. What that really meant was they, the pathologists, thought it was a cancer of a lesser degree, but needed to cover their buttocks with the terminology that it had "follicular tendencies."

One good thing does come from a cancer diagnosis, it makes one realize what is really important in life. As a cancer patient I developed a deeper appreciation of life and slowly learned to let go of the little things. Jerry was so good to me and very supportive. We both gained strength from this ordeal and forged ahead with a greater love and commitment. And, I knew my mother's visit was real. She told me what I needed to know, she gave me the strength I needed to get through the surgery and the treatment.

A few weeks later, I had a thyroid scan done. This revealed the cancer had a 14% spread into my neck. Shortly after that test I was hospitalized for three days in an isolation room. I had to swallow 4 large (horse size) radioactive pills for the treatment. I was not allowed to have any visitors due to the radiation they would be exposed to. I went home after three days but could not hold or hug my husband and children for a week. They couldn't be exposed to the lingering radiation in my system.

Chapter 18

Years passed. The girls were growing like weeds. Kristie was about to enter college, Jessica was in high school and very involved with sports. Jill was my shadow. She was in Junior High, and very close to me.

Jerry and I began to find a new interest in the theater. We had become choral members of a semiprofessional opera company. I have always loved to sing, and my years of playing the guitar and singing with my contemporary folk choir at our Catholic church had given me the confidence I needed to get involved with the theater company. Jerry, on the other, hand had no problem being on stage, pretending to be some character other than himself. He liked being the center of attention and, Jerry being Jerry, would try to always "upstage" me if he had the opportunity. Yes, life was great! Jerry and I really enjoyed being in the musicals and operas. Our girls and friends have had many laughs seeing us up on stage.

My life was very centered on my family. Interestingly, I had no longer thought of David since the day I threw out the letters and pictures. It was as if I had purged myself of him.

In April 1999, I went for my annual mammogram. I no sooner arrived back home when I received a call from one of the doctors I worked for at a family clinic in town. He told me that he received a call from the radiologist telling him something was found on my mammogram. He said I needed to see a surgeon for a biopsy. I couldn't believe what I was hearing. A cold feeling washed over me. I hung up the phone and sat down. I started to hyperventilate. I couldn't sit still. I couldn't read, or watch TV. I felt so anxious that I needed to get out and walk. I needed to clear the cobwebs from my head and think about what this doctor told me on the phone.

Okay Karen, calm down. It's just a biopsy. Let them do this, get it over with and you'll find out it is benign. Don't worry. You already had cancer; this isn't going to happen again.

Well…it did. I was diagnosed with breast cancer. I had a lumpectomy and a five week treatment of radiation.

As I was lying on the table for the rad treatment, I began to realize the pain and discomfort my mother endured with her radiation treatment. She had a stronger dose for her lung cancer and had six weeks of treatment which caused her to suffer with nausea and vomiting, not to mention the burns.

I did relatively well during the most of the radiation treatment. I did feel exhausted by the fifth week but that didn't hold a candle to the burns on my skin from the radiation. I was advised to get some "bag balm" to apply to the burn area. This worked very well. To think a $7.00 jar of bag balm cleared the burns within a day or so, was phenomenal. The ointment was originally used on cow's udders, but became intensely popular with mechanics and other workers whose hands took a lot of abuse. I thought it was a little weird but also hilarious.

After my five weeks of treatment, I started a five year regime of Tamoxifen, a common anti-cancer medication to prevent the return of breast cancer.

Chapter 19

I had been seven years free of cancer when I learned of Aunt Mary's death. It was about a year since the dreams of David began.

Jerry and I had been married thirty two years at the time of my aunt's funeral. We had built years of memories both good and bad. We had experienced joy, sadness, laughter, anger, tears, and lots of love in that time together. We had survived raising three teenage daughters and all the drama that went with it. We had survived two cancer diagnoses and treatments. And of course, we did survive our thirty two years of marriage.

Sometimes I think if Jerry did not have the sense of humor he had, we would not have gotten through some of the rough times. It may not surprise you to learn that he was the "Good Cop" while I had the role of the "Bad Cop" to our children. I was as strict with the girls as my parents were with me and my siblings. Yes, I have to admit, I became my *parents* even though I vowed not to be like them. I may have been too hard on the girls at times, but Jerry always managed to put the trauma of those moments in a lighter light with humor. He always balanced our

"Cop" duties in a way that would make us laugh, including the girls.

They grew up becoming delightful, responsible young women. We were blessed!

After Aunt Mary's funeral, David continued to haunt my dreams. What was this about? I had to find out what was going on. I began my search for David.

I gathered up strength and stopped at David's old home on Morgan Circle. There was, of course, a new owner; an older woman living alone with her dog. I introduced myself as a former neighbor looking for David and John White. She said she did not know very much about the boys, other than that David and John had gone through an extremely rough time after losing their father and then their youngest sister. John had the difficult task of caring for his ailing father. I don't think it was too long after Arnold died that Cindy discovered she had lung cancer, which of course was not a battle she would win. John and David had lost so much. David again was dealing with the demon of alcohol. The woman living at David's old home told me she had heard

David moved to Florida, but did not know where John had gone.

My husband Jerry had known about the dreams, but now I had to tell him something serious was happening. As time went by, I became convinced that I needed to contact David and John. I wasn't exactly sure why, but in my heart, I knew David was in trouble and needed some help. For a year I checked the internet and made phone calls to try to find them. I called an old number I had for John without any success. What was going on in my mind? I felt driven to find these brothers. I knew it had to be done and doing this without knowing the reason behind it was strange to say the least. I had to do this. I had to trust. I had to have faith.

Chapter 20

In January of 2007, I was still searching for David and John. I decided to try one simple little thing and called information to find if there was a John White in the Springfield, MA area. I was given four numbers. I called three of them without any luck, and then on the fourth try, a woman with a kind voice answered the phone. I asked her if she was Mrs. John White. Skeptically, she replied yes. I asked if she was married to John, from Gilford, MA and brother to David age fifty nine. She said yes. I explained to her who I was, saying I was a neighbor growing up with the Whites' and had been trying to contact them for a couple of years.

She introduced herself as Peggy. She named John's parents, Mary and Arnold, his sister Cindy and their home address, on Morgan Circle. Yes, this is the family I've been looking for. I was so excited! Peggy and I talked for a little while. John was not at home at that time, but Peggy said she would have John call me when he returned that night. I was at a church meeting when John called me, so I did not get to talk with him then. However, I did reach him the next night.

We talked for an hour or so, catching up on the old times. I tried to explain to John, with great difficulty, why I was looking for David. I did not want to sound like an idiot or crazy lady but still felt a pressing need to reach David. John said all he knew was that David was living in Florida. He did not know where, nor had he heard from him in ten years. I could hear the sadness and frustration in his voice. I was disappointed when John asked me to hold off in my pursuit. For whatever reason, I agreed to wait a little while, but not too long, as I felt the need to find David was becoming urgent.

John and I talked on the phone every few weeks for several months. It was early in November of 2007 when I called John again and said,

"This is it, buddy. I have to find David, have you heard anything yet?"

Again he said no. So, once again I was back on the Internet.

Do you believe in miracles? John called me one week later. He had heard from David. David was in a hospice facility in Florida. He had lung cancer which had metastasized to his brain. John was now convinced of my need to reach David. John called David and told him I had been searching for him and asked if it would be alright if I called him. David said,

"Yes, give her my number." and said he looked forward to hearing from me.
John and Peggy would be flying down to see him that next week. John said he would fill me in on the details of their trip when he got back.

I told Jerry what had developed. John had heard from David and David was dying.

David had had emergency surgery to try to remove the tumor on his brain. I was still trying to make sense of the last few years and this driving goal to find David. Now that I did, what was I to do? The first question Jerry asked me was,

"Are you going down to see him?"

I froze for a moment, took a deep breath, and looked deeply into my husband eyes.

"I don't know," I said, "I hadn't really thought it through. How would you feel if I did?" I asked. "Is this something you would agree to?"

Neither one of us knew the answer to that question, at least for that moment.

Chapter 21

John and Peggy returned from their visit
with David. Needless to say, it was an
emotional reunion. The ten years lost
between these two brothers who loved each
other, who had been so deeply affected by
losing their parents and youngest sister was
more than they could bear. David, in effect,
hid himself in Florida where he had no
reminders of his past. John had moved on
with his life, having met Peggy and falling
in love again. He was brave enough to
remarry and build a new life with the
woman he was meant to be with. David
lived these past ten years finding new
friends, working a new job, and staying
away from romantic relationships. He
sobered up and straightened out his life, all
without any ties to his home town.

I spoke with David numerous times on the
phone. It was strange, yet easy to talk with
him. It was as if thirty six years had not
gone by. Hearing his voice was so
comforting, but also emotional. I think I
could hear his voice break and I tried so
hard to keep from crying as we continued to
speak. I don't remember if he asked me to
go to see him, or if I asked the question. All

I know is my husband charged my airline
ticket on his credit card and told me to go.
How ironic that I was flying to see the
person I flew away from some thirty six
years ago. There I was on my way to
Florida, renting a car and driving myself on
the Florida turnpike to an unfamiliar
destination to see the man who had stolen
my heart as a teenager.

I found the hospice two hours later than I
expected. I was using the recently invented
navigation system that kept saying,

"RECALCULATING".

I had taken so many wrong turns on the
turnpike because I was always in the wrong
lane. What was that promise I made to
myself in the 70's? That I would not travel
in unknown places alone? Finally I walked
into a fairly new building that looked like a
large beautiful, sprawling ranch. I was
directed to room # 7 (my lucky number). As
I walked into the room, I saw David
standing and cleaning his glasses. I
suddenly felt panicky. After all, I had gained
a fair amount of weight these last few years.
Although my graying hair was highlighted,
it did not necessarily camouflage my age.

I had changed, and in my opinion, not for the better.

As I entered his room, I said hello. He said hello, thinking I was one of his nurses. I whispered a quiet hello again with a soft smile on my face. He looked over at me and smiled his same old loving smile. We embraced. He looked wonderful, far better than I expected. His hair was growing in from the surgery, although it was now quite gray instead of the dark brown hair he had in his youth. His eyes were as blue as I remembered them and his smile had that same playful twist it always had. He was thin, but not too thin, and he wore glasses just as I wore glasses. We talked, and talked, and talked. It was so good to be with him, to see him again after all these years.

I told him about my family, and about my grandson Jonathan, the newest love of my life. We talked about our parents, our home town, our youth, and the love we had shared. I couldn't help but ask him why he didn't come after me, what seemed a lifetime ago. I couldn't help but ask him why he got married so soon. His answer simply was,

"I screwed up."

He said he didn't think I loved him when I left for California even though I had sworn to him I did. He was convinced by his cousins, and *new girlfriend* that I was gone for good. What could we say? The past was in the past. We couldn't change it. I wouldn't have changed it, not without throwing away the life I had built with my husband and children. No, what was meant to be, had been. We were now dealing with the reality of the present time, which was the closing chapter in his life.

We left his room and walked slowly down the hall holding hands. We stopped at the nurse's station and he introduced me to the nurses and his friends as "his sweetheart." Then we continued to walk towards the lobby where the Christmas tree was decorated.

I arrived three days after Thanksgiving, but we were definitely into the Christmas season. We sat in front of the cozy fireplace feeling the warmth of the fire. It seemed strange to see the green trees outside with seventy- degree temperatures, but it was Florida after all. Back home in Massachusetts, the temperature was dipping below forty degrees and snow was not too far away.

I thought about Jerry and wondered what he was doing. I thought about our girls and couldn't believe how each one of them encouraged me to go visit David. How lucky was I to have the family I had, and here was David alone in the hospice. Oh, his nurses were wonderful. They did become his family. He got the best care anyone could get, and yet, I wanted to bring him home. I wanted to make his illness go away. I wanted him to have some happiness and not the loneliness he had endured for a good part of his life. That of course, was impossible and unrealistic. He was terminal. He knew it and I knew it. There was nothing I could do to change it. He seemed to accept this, however. He was either brave or putting on a brave front for me.

That night, I stayed at the hospice with David. I fell asleep on an extremely uncomfortable fold-out chair as he watched TV. I awoke every now and then and asked him if I was snoring. He politely said no. I'm sure he lied. When I awoke again, he was sleeping in his twin-size hospital bed. I walked over to the sink in his room to wash my face and fix my hair. I heard him say,

"You're still beautiful."

Then he closed his pale blue eyes and again fell asleep. I watched him breathe and said a prayer of thanks for letting me arrive safely to see him again and to spend my "three days with David."

As he slept, I found my second wind. I went out to speak with the nurses. I needed to get a better understanding of his condition. They were vague, even though David had given them permission to speak candidly with me.

"He has been doing very well," they said.

He was having headaches, which were being controlled by his medication. They were concerned about him after one nurse heard him talking to the television.

"Oh Pooh," I said, with a chuckle, "I talk to the freaking television too!"

We all laughed and decided that was not an issue. David would get tired easily and had days when walking was a bit difficult. But for the three weeks he was there, he had been recovering remarkably from his surgery. No one could predict the time he had left. He could have a major seizure or go into a coma and peacefully move on.

I wanted to make our three days together as comforting and happy as I possibly could.

The next day, I left the hospice to do some shopping for David. I stopped to get some pictures developed for him and enlarged a favorite one he had of his big tractor. He was so proud of that green monster. "It even had air conditioning," he said. I checked into a small motel about eight miles away from the hospice house. I took a shower, rested on a comfortable king-size bed, and fell asleep for an hour or so. Before I returned to see David, I stopped at one of the fast food restaurants to grab a bite of supper.

When I arrived back at hospice house, I found David having his dinner and watching one of his favorite television stations, The Discovery Channel. I showed him the pictures I had developed at the store and put them into a photo album I bought for him. After he ate, we walked out onto the screened porch and sat at the round glass patio table with some of his hospice companions. All too soon, however, it was time for me to go back to my motel room and let David have some rest.

As I drove to the motel, I thought about the last few days, and how this trip transpired so quickly. I had taken three personal days off from work to be with David. I was afraid to put this trip off till Christmas for fear that his time may be running out. I was so lucky to have been given the time off from my job at the medical practice where I worked. My supervisor, Belinda, was very understanding and quite gracious in giving me the time away that I needed. I was also amazed how much I missed Jerry in just the two days I had been away.

I arrived at my motel room and called my husband. I just needed to hear his voice and ask how the girls were. It was so comforting to hear him. I told him about the beautiful home David was in and wonderful care he was getting. I wondered if I could have let Jerry go off to visit an "old flame" if the situation were reversed? It was time to say goodnight. I turned off the light and quickly fell asleep.

The next morning I jumped into the shower, checked out of the motel, and stopped to get some breakfast at "Cinnamon Sticks," a terrific little restaurant with a wonderful bakery. David so raved about the apple pie, that I just had to buy one for him. When I walked into his room, his eyes lit up like a Christmas tree when I told him I bought the pie. You would have thought he won the lottery. David was sure to keep that pie for himself. That pie box went into the refrigerator with his name on it, not to be touched by any other person, including myself.

That day was more difficult for David. He was on the quiet side, and not wanting to walk around very much. I later learned that it was one of his bad days. His balance was off and his legs were weak. We stayed in his room for most of the day watching TV and napping. We sent out for pizza that night for supper. The pizzas were okay, but not great. I wish I had known the area better so I could have taken David out to eat, but again, he was not comfortable or strong enough to venture out. I stayed that night at Hospice House with David because I had to leave early the next morning for the airport. We sat and talked more about our past. I saw the sadness in his eyes and I knew he could see the sadness in mine. I took his hands into my hands and said,

You mean so much to me. We can't beat ourselves up for what was and what was not. Our lives were meant to go in different directions, for whatever reasons. I just want you to know, I truly loved you and you are a good person. You will always be in my heart.

My thoughts drifted to the song "Ain't No Mountain." I had kept my promise to David. I had gone to him when he needed me.

We held hands for a moment longer, and then I got up to go out for some air. I sat out on the screened porch. One of David's nurses came out for a cigarette break.

May I have one of those crappy things? I asked, as I was trying to keep from crying.

Yes, I knew these are what caused David's lung cancer; I knew it caused my mothers, his mother's and his sister's lung cancer. It was either smoke a cigarette at that moment or have a drink and since there was no alcohol on the premises (or Boones Farm for that matter); the cigarette was my only option. That was my last cigarette as I was not really a smoker. I had quit smoking back in 1972 after my mother died.

This nurse, Donna, was friendly, pretty and about fifteen years younger than I. She sat with me for a while, letting me shed the tears I had been holding back. She listened to me chatter on about nothing. She was just what I needed at that moment. She was someone who listened. She was someone who cared.

After I got myself together, I went back to David's room. He wanted to watch some TV show I had no interest in, so I snoozed till he went to sleep in his bed. I couldn't sleep on that horrible pull-out again, so I sat in David's recliner, leaned back, and slept peacefully through the night.

Wednesday morning David woke me at 7:00 AM. I had to drive back to Orlando Airport to catch my 11:00 AM flight. We ate some breakfast, and then I walked down to the ladies room to wash up and change into some comfortable traveling clothes. I went back to his room, where he was waiting for me. We hugged. I kissed him on the cheek as we said our goodbyes. He walked me outside and said,

"No tears now."

Hearing his words, quickly brought back the memories of sobbing in his arms when he left to go overseas.

I summoned up a smile and said, "Of course not." I walked toward my rented car and turned to look at him again.

"Love you," I said, without thinking.

"I love you too," he said.

"Always have and always will."

I wanted to run back and jump into his arms but knew if I did that, I would probably have knocked him over and killed him. So instead, I gave him my biggest smile, got in the car, and drove away, waving my last wave to him. I drove down the street, stopped the car and cried like a baby.

Okay, enough now Karen. You have to get yourself to the airport on time to catch your flight. You can't drive on the turnpike with a flood of tears running from your eyes. Get yourself together now. It's time to go home.

Chapter 22

My flight landed on time. Jerry was there to pick me up. He kissed me and asked how my trip was. I smiled and said,

"Sad, but nice."

Nothing more was said at that time. We had to get to the opera as we were now board members of the opera company in our town. This was opening night for "Rigoletto."

I don't remember seeing too much of the opera. I fell asleep in my bumpy uncomfortable theater seat. I was just glad we were not in this production. I can't imagine what would have happened if I fell asleep on stage. Jerry and I went directly home after the opera, and I quickly crawled into bed.

Weeks went by. David and I spoke frequently on the phone. David celebrated his Sixtieth Birthday on the Nineteenth of December. I called to wish him a Happy Birthday and asked how he was feeling. He said he was feeling fine and was about to have his favorite cake, a pistachio cake that the chef at the Hospice House had made for him. Before saying goodbye, I told David I would talk with him in a few days.

We spoke every two or three days. Sometimes he sounded great other times he sounded tired. Christmas and New Year's came and went. I finally developed the pictures I had taken while visiting David. I had a special picture enlarged. It was a picture of the two of us in his room the night we ordered pizzas.

I called him on Thursday, January 17, 2008, early in the morning. His nurse answered and said,

"Let me see if he is up and able to talk with you."

David picked up the phone and said, "Hello Karen," in what I thought was a tired, morning voice.

I told him I was mailing him a card with a special picture in it, and please watch for it to arrive. He said

"I'm not going anywhere." He replied,

"Bye for now, I will call you tomorrow."

That next day when I got home from work, my daughter Jill told me there was a message on the phone from David's brother John. As I listened, my hand began to shake and again the tears flowed. David had passed away at 2:00 that morning.

"He was comfortable and had his devoted nurses by his side," John said.

Jillian was quick to wrap her arms around me. She said,

"I'm sorry, Mom."

I walked into the bathroom, washed my face and took a deep breath to compose myself. I did not return John's call that night, as I knew it would be too emotional for us to talk. Jerry came home from work, saw the look on my face, and said,

"You knew this was going to happen, honey"

"Of course," I said. "I just wished he had more time."

The next day I spoke with John. We spoke for quite a while; we cried, we laughed, and comforted each other over the phone.

Although John originally did not think I should have gone to see David, he spoke of how glad he was that I did go. He said that it meant a lot to David that I was there. All I knew was that something or someone kept after me to find David. We all think Mary, his mother, was behind it, but nonetheless, I did what I had to do, and I don't regret it.

John had finally told me that David did have his problems with alcohol, but also had a sex addiction. He was told by David that his involvement with other women meant nothing to him. John said David's life spiraled down after I left him. He never really got himself together, nor could he maintain relationships. David's departure to Florida was one of the things he did right for himself. David did stop drinking and womanizing. John did say something I will never forget. He told me that I was the "Love of David's Life."

I was so very sorry I could not have helped David overcome his addictions early on. I was neither strong enough nor mature enough.

I often wondered how Jerry could be so supportive about my visit with David, so I once asked him.

Why did you let me go to see David?

He said,

"You would have done it regardless."

I told him that was not true. I could not, nor would not, have gone without his support.

He then said,

"I know you want to pave your pathway to heaven…"

I interrupted him, telling him he was full of crap. Jerry finally confessed. He said;

"If he should ever hear that his old girlfriend was suffering from a terminal hangnail, then he would expect me to allow him to go to visit her."

Now, I ask you, how I could ever refuse?

He made me laugh, again, as always, my husband of thirty three years!

Epilogue

Ten years have passed since my dreams of David and the journey to find him began. Seven years have passed since David's death. I think of David every day, and I'm so grateful that I had the chance to spend my three days with him. The pain and loneliness I experienced with him in my younger years had all washed away. I remember David fondly, and with love.

I was inspired to write about David because I was personally surprised, not only by the dreams and how they compelled me to find David, but also how I sensed he was in need of help.

The timing of all the events; the dreams, the countless phone calls to families in Florida, finding John when I did, and my finally finding David, seemed to be a frustrating mess at the time. But now, in retrospect it all falls into place. It all makes sense.

My husband, Jerry, supported me in my endeavor, although he thought I was being a bit nutty. My three daughters, Kristine, Jessica, and Jillian gave me the encouragement I needed to continue searching in spite of the fact that I had no idea what the final outcome would be.

My two sisters, Wendy and Marilyn, and two brothers, Tim and Mike, gave me the strength to start my search, and the fortitude to continue with it.

My faith in God and my past spiritual experiences empowered me to find David. And, once again proved to me that with God, all things are possible.

I hope my story will encourage each and every one of you to listen to the spirit within you. Keep an open mind to the subtle hints that surround you. Even more important, find the courage to pursue and walk the path that is spiritually revealed to you.

About the Author

Karen Faszcza lives in the small town of Florence MA, with her husband, Jerry, and two dogs, Kayla and Bella. Her passions include playing guitar and singing in a contemporary folk group for the past thirty plus years. She adores spending time with her husband, three daughters, and especially her three grandchildren, Jonathan, Alexa and Jackson. Karen cherishes her strong and unique friends, Judy, Pat, Carol, Lorraine, Noreen, Jan, Gail, Susanne and many more. Karen enjoys reading and travelling. She was raised a Catholic and continues to practice her faith. She truly believes in spiritual paths, spiritual guides and Guardian Angels. She hopes that this story conveys that message.

Made in the USA
Middletown, DE
20 April 2016